Martial Arts
Karate Punches

by Stuart Schwartz
and Craig Conley

Consultant:
Mark Willie, Instructor
Central Minnesota Karate
Mankato State University

C A P S T O N E
H I G H / L O W B O O K S
an imprint of Capstone Press
Mankato, Minnesota

Capstone High/Low Books are published by Capstone Press
818 North Willow Street • Mankato, MN 56001
http://www.capstone-press.com

Library of Congress Cataloging-in-Publication Data
Schwartz, Stuart, 1945–
Karate punches/by Stuart Schwartz and Craig Conley.
p. cm.—(Martial arts)
Includes bibliographical references (p. 44) and index.
Summary: A general description of karate, including its origins and
development, warm-up exercises, basic and advanced punches, and safety
aspects.
ISBN 0-7368-0011-5
1. Karate—Juvenile literature. [1. Karate.] I. Conley, Craig, 1965– . II. Title.
III. Series: Martial arts (Mankato, Minn.)
GV1114.3.S359   1999
796.815—dc21
                                              98-18601
                                                 CIP
                                                  AC

Editorial Credits

Cara Van Voorst, editor; James Franklin, cover designer and illustrator;
  Sheri Gosewisch, photo researcher

Photo Credits

All photographs by Gallery 19/Gregg R. Andersen.

Table of Contents

Chapter 1

Learning Karate

Karate is a form of self-defense. Self-defense is the act of protecting oneself from harm. Karate means empty hand in Japanese. Karate students use only their hands and feet as weapons. They combine arm and leg movements to defend themselves. They perform blocks, kicks, strikes, and punches.

A karate-ka is a karate student. Almost anyone can become a karate-ka. Beginning karate-ka should check with doctors before practicing karate. Doctors make sure the students are healthy enough for training.

Shotokan Karate
People on Okinawa Island near Japan developed karate in the 1600s.

Karate students use their hands and feet for self-defense.

A dojo has a large room with mirrors on the walls.

Karate is a martial art that is a style of self-defense or fighting. Many martial arts come from Asia.

People in different areas of Okinawa and Japan soon developed their own styles of karate. Gichin Funakoshi developed the Shotokan style of karate. Many karate-ka consider Funakoshi the Father of Modern Karate. He taught karate on Okinawa Island in the early 1900s. Then the Emperor of Japan asked Funakoshi to demonstrate karate at his palace. The emperor liked karate. He asked Funakoshi to open a karate school in 1922. Funakoshi taught his Shotokan style to Japanese people until his death in 1957. This book describes Shotokan-style movements.

People in North America first learned karate from a Japanese sensei (SEN-say) named Oshima. A sensei is a teacher.

People in North America liked karate as a sport. Today, many karate-ka participate in karate competitions. A competition is a contest of skill. People around the world learn karate for self-defense and for sport.

Places to Practice

Most karate-ka practice karate in dojos. A dojo is a karate school. Many cities and towns around the world have dojos. A dojo has a large, open room with mirrors on its walls. The karate-ka need the open room to practice basic

movements. They look at themselves in the mirrors to make sure they are practicing movements correctly.

Karate-ka can practice anywhere there is open space. For example, some karate-ka practice movements outside. Other karate-ka practice in large rooms at their homes.

Karate Punches

Karate-ka learn blocks, kicks, strikes, and punches for self-defense. This book describes common karate punches.

Karate-ka use punches to attack opponents. An opponent is someone against whom a karate-ka is fighting. Karate-ka can punch any area of a body that is not blocked. Some punches are more effective on certain areas of the body.

Karate-ka choose to use a punch instead of a strike when they want a forceful attack. A punch is a thrusting movement. Strikes are quick, snapping movements.

Karate-ka can punch any area of the body that is not blocked.

Chapter 2

Warming Up

Karate-ka warm up before they practice karate. They warm up to help prevent injuries to joints or muscles.

Any loose-fitting clothing works well for karate practice. Most karate-ka wear loose-fitting, cotton uniforms called gi (GEE) for karate practice. Karate-ka tie their gi with belts. Different colored belts show the skill levels of the students. Beginning karate-ka wear white belts. The most advanced karate-ka wear black belts.

Karate-ka stretch their necks, arms, and upper bodies before practicing punches. They perform neck rotations, arm rotations, and body rotations. A rotation is a circular

Most karate-ka wear gi for karate practice.

movement. Karate-ka also perform body stretches to warm up.

Karate-ka practice each warm-up at least five times. These warm-ups relax and prepare the muscles for practice.

Neck and Arm Rotations

Neck rotations loosen the neck muscles. A karate-ka begins a neck rotation by tipping her head to the right. Then she rolls her head to the front and to the left in a circular motion. The karate-ka then rolls her head from the left to the back. She completes one full neck rotation by rolling her head back to the right. She then does the movement in the other direction.

Arm rotations help loosen shoulder and arm muscles. The karate-ka begins arm rotations by standing with her feet shoulder width apart. Then she swings her arm up and backward in a circle. She does the movement with both arms. She also does the movement in the other direction.

A karate-ka does a body rotation to loosen her stomach muscles.

Body Rotations and Body Stretches

Body rotations help stretch waist and hip muscles. The karate-ka begins body rotations by standing with her feet shoulder width apart and her hands on her hips. She slowly twists her upper body to the right. She then twists her upper body to the left.

A karate-ka stands with his hands on his hips to begin a body stretch. His feet are about shoulder width apart. He clasps his hands above his head and stretches his arms as far as he can. The karate-ka keeps his hands above his head and bends to each side.

A karate-ka clasps his hands over his head and bends to each side during a body stretch.

Chapter 3

Basic Punches

A punch is a powerful hand and arm movement. A karate-ka thrusts his hand and arm to deliver a punch.

A beginning karate-ka learns three basic punches. These punches are the straight punch, the reverse punch, and the lunge punch. He practices punching with both arms. The punches described in this book are right arm punches.

Stances
Stances are the basis of every movement in karate. A karate-ka learns these standing positions at the beginning of her karate training. Two common stances for punches are the front stance and the straddle-leg stance. But a karate-ka can deliver a punch from most stances.

A punch is a powerful hand and arm movement.

Front Stance

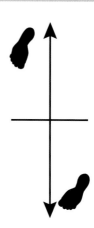

Straddle-leg Stance

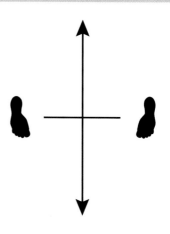

A karate-ka begins a front stance by stepping forward with one leg. She bends her front knee and keeps her back leg straight. The knee of her front leg is directly over her front foot. Her feet are shoulder width apart. She keeps her back straight. The karate-ka can face her upper body forward or turn it to the side.

A karate-ka stands with his legs out to his sides in the straddle-leg stance. His feet are two shoulder widths apart and point forward. He turns his knees slightly outward and bends them. His knees do not bend outward past his feet.

Fist Position and Withdrawn Position

A karate-ka forms a fist for most punches. She forms a fist from an open hand. She curls her fingers so her fingertips touch the bottoms of her fingers. She continues to bend her fingers and presses them into her palm. She then presses her thumb across her index finger and middle finger.

Most punches begin with the fist in a withdrawn position. The withdrawn position is

A karate-ka keeps her fists near her waist in the withdrawn position.

near the waist slightly above the hips. The backs of her fists face the floor. She points her elbows backward.

Straight Punch

A karate-ka can perform a straight punch with his right or left arm. He can aim a straight punch to an opponent's head, chest, or stomach.

A karate-ka begins a right straight punch with his left arm straight out in front of his chest. His right hand is in the withdrawn position.

The karate-ka pulls his left hand into the withdrawn position. He thrusts his right hand outward in a straight path toward the target. The karate-ka rotates his wrist inward before he completes the punch. He hits the target with the knuckles on his middle and index fingers. He holds his wrist straight.

Reverse Punch

A karate-ka often practices a reverse punch by starting in the front stance position. A karate-ka stands with her left leg forward to do a right reverse punch. She holds her left arm straight out in front of her body. She turns her hips 45 degrees to her right side. Her right fist is in the withdrawn position.

Next, she thrusts her right hand forward. She rotates her hips and shoulders forward at the same time. She rotates her wrist inward and hits the target with the knuckles of her index and middle fingers. She pulls her left hand into the withdrawn position.

Lunge Punch

A lunge punch is more powerful than a reverse punch. To lunge means to move forward quickly. This lunging motion adds power to a lunge punch.

A karate-ka begins a lunge punch with his right fist in the withdrawn position. He places his left arm straight out in front of his body.

He pulls his left fist into the withdrawn position as he punches with his right fist. He lunges forward by stepping into a front stance with his right foot. He delivers a straight punch with his right arm as he steps forward.

A lunge punch is more powerful than a reverse punch.

Chapter 4

Advanced Punches

A karate-ka learns advanced punches after he can perform the basic punches easily. An advanced karate-ka learns the round punch and the hook punch. He also learns the double punch, the uppercut punch, and the U-punch.

Round Punch and Hook Punch

The round punch and the hook punch are similar movements. A karate-ka begins a round punch with her right fist in the withdrawn position. Her left arm is straight out in front of her body.

She pulls her left fist into the withdrawn position. At the same time, she pushes her right arm slightly out to the side. She swings her arm around toward her opponent. She

A karate-ka swings her arm around toward her opponent during a round punch.

Start

Finish

A karate-ka aims a hook punch to the area in front of his chest.

rotates her wrist inward before her fist hits the target. She hits the target with the knuckles of her index and middle fingers.

A karate-ka also begins a right hook punch with his left arm straight out in front of his body. His right fist is in the withdrawn position.

He pulls his left fist into the withdrawn position. At the same time, he moves his right

Start

Finish

A karate-ka can do a double punch with both fists side by side.

fist forward and to the left. He keeps his elbow bent throughout the punch. He rotates his wrist inward as he punches to the left. He aims his punch to the area in front of his chest.

Double Punch

A karate-ka uses both hands for a double punch. A double punch begins with both hands in the withdrawn position. The karate-ka steps

27

Start Finish

A karate-ka also can do a double punch with one fist above the other fist.

into a front stance. He thrusts both fists forward at the same time. The karate-ka aims at the target straight in front of him. He keeps both fists side by side throughout the punch.

A karate-ka also can do a double punch with one fist above the other fist. The thumbs of both fists must face each other.

The uppercut punch is most effective when an opponent is close.

Uppercut Punch

The uppercut punch is most effective when an opponent is close. A karate-ka begins an uppercut punch with his right fist in the withdrawn position. His left arm is straight out in front of him. He pulls his left arm into the withdrawn position. At the same time, he

thrusts his right fist forward. He keeps his arm bent at a 90-degree angle throughout the punch.

The karate-ka aims at his opponent's chin with the knuckles of his index and middle fingers. The palm of his fist faces himself.

U-Punch

A U-punch is similar to a double punch. But a karate-ka puts her left fist above her right fist. The backs of both fists face to her right side. She turns her arms so her right shoulder is lower than her left shoulder.

Her left arm is over her head. She aims at an opponent's stomach with her lower fist. She aims at her opponent's head with her upper fist.

A karate-ka aims at an opponent's stomach with her lower fist and at his head with her upper fist during a U-punch.

Chapter 5

Safety and Training

Safety is an important part of karate training. Karate-ka have to follow rules to stay safe. Most karate dojos have rules about how to groom, warm up, condition, and control movements. To groom means to take care of one's appearance and clothing. To condition means to exercise to stay fit. Karate-ka also wear protective gear for some parts of karate training.

Karate-ka must respect their instructor and other students as part of their training. Students bow to their instructor before and after class. They also bow to their partners before and after sparring matches. Sparring

Karate-ka have to follow rules to stay safe.

means to practice fighting. Karate students bow to show respect for one another.

Shotokan-style karate is low-contact karate. This means karate-ka keep their punches, strikes, and kicks from hitting their opponents. Karate-ka have less chance of hurting themselves and others during low-contact karate.

Grooming

Karate-ka need to keep their bodies and gi clean. This is important because sweat and dirt can cause and spread illness. Karate-ka must go to class clean and shower after they practice karate.

Karate-ka need to trim and clean their fingernails and toenails. Long nails can scratch people. Karate-ka also must tie back long hair during practice. They might not see kicks or strikes if they have hair in their faces.

Karate-ka remove their watches and jewelry before practicing. Karate-ka wearing jewelry could hurt themselves or others. For example, a karate-ka could tear an earring out of

Karate-ka bow to their partners before and after sparring matches to show respect.

someone's ear. Or a student could scratch another karate-ka with a ring or a watch.

Warming Up and Conditioning
Karate-ka must warm up before they practice. Students stretch to help prevent injuries. Karate-ka might pull or rip muscles if they do not warm up before practicing movements.

Karate-ka condition themselves by lifting weights and jogging. Exercises strengthen their hearts, muscles, and lungs. Karate-ka who are fit are less likely to hurt themselves.

Fit karate-ka also can practice karate longer without becoming tired and careless. Careless karate-ka might perform movements wrong and hurt themselves. Or they might lose control of movements and accidentally hurt someone else.

Sparring

Many karate-ka train so they can spar. Two karate-ka compete in a sparring match. The person who scores the most points wins the match. Karate-ka earn points when they come close to hitting certain areas of their opponents' bodies.

Karate-ka must follow rules for sparring. These rules lower the chances of karate-ka hurting each other. There are different rules for low-contact sparring and high-contact sparring.

Karate-ka must follow rules for sparring.

Karate-ka in low-contact sparring must try to stop their punches before they hit their opponents. Karate-ka try to stop about one inch (2.5 centimeters) from their opponents.

Some karate styles practice high-contact sparring. These students still need to control their movements. They can only hit their opponents in areas that are protected by pads.

Protective Gear

Karate school officials require karate-ka to wear protective gear during sparring. Shotokan karate-ka must wear mouth guards during sparring. A mouth guard protects the teeth. An accidental kick or punch to the mouth could knock out unprotected teeth.

Karate-ka also wear padded gloves. Padded gloves cover the hands over the knuckles. The gloves protect the hands during strikes and punches. Gloves also soften blows to and from opponents.

Karate-ka need additional protective gear when they practice high-contact sparring.

All karate-ka must wear mouth guards and padded gloves when they spar.

This padded gear protects the body from hits. Karate-ka may wear helmets, chest protectors, forearm guards, shin guards, and foot gloves.

Karate is an exciting sport. But it can be dangerous if people do not follow the rules. Beginning students should not try to perform advanced movements before they master basic movements. Advanced students should continue to practice basic movements. Practice and patience will help a karate-ka master karate skills safely.

Practice and patience will help a karate-ka learn karate skills safely.

Words to Know

competition (kom-puh-TISH-uhn)—a contest of skill

condition (kuhn-DISH-uhn)—exercise daily to keep the body fit

dojo (DOH-joh)—a karate school

gi (GEE)—a loose-fitting, cotton uniform

groom (GROOM)—to take care of appearance and clothing

injury (IN-juh-ree)—harm to the body

karate-ka (kah-RAH-tee-kah)—a karate student

martial art (MAR-shuhl ART)—a style of self-defense and fighting

rotation (roh-TAY-shuhn)—a circular motion made by a body part

self-defense (SELF-di-FENSS)—the act of protecting oneself

sensei (SEN-say)—a teacher

spar (SPAHR)—to practice fighting

Many people learn karate for self-defense.

To Learn More

Corrigan, Ralph. *Karate Made Easy*. New York: Sterling Publications, 1995.

Gutman, Bill. *Karate*. Minneapolis: Capstone Press, 1995.

Leder, Jane Mersky. *Karate*. Learning How. Marco, Fla.: Bancroft-Sage Publishing, 1992.

Queen, J. Allen. *Start Karate!* New York: Sterling Publications, 1997.

Sieh, Ron. *Martial Arts for Beginners*. New York: Writers and Readers, 1995.

A white belt learns a self-defense move from his instructor.

Useful Addresses

Canadian Shotokan Karate Association
1646 McPherson Drive
Port Coquitlam, BC V3C 6C9
Canada

**International Society of
  Okinawan/Japanese Karate-Do**
21512 Sherman Way
Canoga Park, CA 91303

Shotokan Karate of America
2500 South La Cienega Boulevard
Los Angeles, CA 90034

World Federation Karate Organization
9506 Las Tunas Drive
Temple City, CA 91780

Internet Sites

Canadian Shotokan Karate Association
http://www.geocities.com/colosseum/field/
  7270

Martial Arts Resource Page
http://www.middlebury.edu/~jswan/
  martial.arts/ma.html

Shotokan Karate for Everyone
http://members.aol.com/edl12/shotokan/
  index.htm

Shotokan Karate of America
http://www.ska.org/

Index